My Day at School

By Alice Proctor

Copyright © ticktock Entertainment Ltd 2007
First published in Great Britain in 2007 by ticktock Media Ltd.,
Unit 2, Orchard Business Centre, North Farm Road,
Tunbridge Wells, Kent, TN2 3XF

ticktock project editor: Julia Adams
ticktock project designer: Emma Randall
ticktock picture researcher: Lizzie Knowles

We would like to thank: Jo Hanks, Debra Voege, Colin Beer, Rebecca Clunes

ISBN 978 1 84696 481 7 pbk

Printed in China

Picture credits
t = top, b = bottom, c = centre, l = left, r = right, OFC = outside front cover, OBC = outside back cover

Alamy: (Image Source Black)1, 19t. Alamy/Stockbyte Silver: OFCr. Banana Stock: 13t. Corbis: 9l, 19b,
OBCbr. Reflexstock: 17t. Shutterstock: 9b, 12, 13b, 15, 20, 21. Superstock: 4l, 8b, 9t, 10, 11, 14, 16,
17b, OBCtr, OBCcr. ticktock Media Archive: 4r, 5, 6, 7, 8r, 24, OFCl, OBCl, OBC far right x3.

Page 22-23 from top left to bottom right: shutterstock, shutterstock, banana stock, shutterstock, Alamy, Corbis,
Shutterstock, Superstock, Shutterstock, shutterstock, superstock, ticktock media archive, ticktock media archive,
shutterstock, shutterstock.

Every effort has been made to trace the copyright holders, and we apologise in advance for any
unintentional omissions. We would be pleased to insert the appropriate acknowledgements in
any subsequent edition of this publication.

Contents

Words in **bold** are explained in the glossary!

Telling the time

Tomorrow is my first day back at school after the holidays. I am so excited!

Let's see if we can tell the time, so we know when it is playtime and lunchtime.

Hours and minutes

The little hand is called the **hour** hand. Here it is pointing at the 3.

The big hand is called the **minute** hand. It is pointing at the 12, so the time is exactly 3 **o'clock**.

There are 60 minutes in an hour.

Let's find out the time on these clocks.

The little hand is pointing at the 10.
The big hand is pointing at the 12.

What time is it?

Look at the hands on this clock.

Where is the little hand pointing?
Where is the big hand pointing?

What time is it?

Do you have a clock or watch?

It is half-past

Not all lessons at school start exactly on the hour. Let's see what happens when the big hand points at the 6.

Half-past 10

Look! The little hand is past the 10. It is half way between the 10 and 11.

The big hand is now pointing at the 6.

The time is **half-past** 10.

It is called half-past because the big hand has moved half way around the clock face.

Half-past 5

The little hand has passed the 5. The big hand pointing at the 6 tells us it is half-past 5.

Digital clocks

Digital clocks have no hands. The first number tells us the hour is 7. The second number tells us it is 30 minutes past 7. This means it is half-past 7. Half an hour is 30 minutes.

Half-past 7 is also called seven-thirty.

My day at school

Today is Monday and I am going back to school. I can't wait to see all of my friends again.

Time to get up

7 o'clock
The alarm clock is ringing.
It must be time to get up.
First it is time for breakfast.
Today we have lots of fresh fruit and some juice.

Getting ready

Half-past 7

After breakfast, I brush my teeth.
Then I get dressed and ready for school.

Off to school

8 o'clock

Mum and I walk to the bus stop. On the way we meet my friend Emma. Quick, I can see the bus coming!

What time do you get up in the morning?

My first lesson

When we get to school, we go into our classroom. Our teacher is there waiting for us and smiling.

Ready to learn?

9 o'clock
Our teacher calls out our names to see who is here.

First of all, we have a spelling quiz. I only make 2 mistakes.

Then it is time to start our maths lesson. Yippee! Today we learn how to add numbers.

Computer sums

10 o'clock

We have done lots of sums. Now it is time to try them on the computer.

Playtime

Half-past 10
Time for a break. Let's go outside to play!

How long is your break at school?

My science lesson

Our break is over after half an hour. Now it is time for our science lesson.

Mini beasts

11 o'clock
Our teacher has a box of creatures to show us.

Spiders have eight legs.

Ladybirds have six legs.

Worms have no legs at all!

On safari...

Half-past 11

Half an hour later we go outside and we look for more mini beasts. Look what I found!

We wash our hands when we finish.

Pasta surprise!

12 o'clock

Emma and I pick spaghetti for lunch. It reminds us of the worms we've just been looking at... yuk!

Afternoon lessons

After our lunch break we are ready to learn even more. Today it is English and art.

Reading and writing

1 o'clock
First it is time to read. I choose my favourite book from the library.

Next we all write a story. Our teacher wants us to give it a surprise ending. I write about a trip to the planet Mars.

Art class

2 o'clock

Today we are painting. I draw a picture of me and my dad in the park.

Remember, an hour is 60 minutes.

My school day ends

When our art class is over, we all get together for our last lesson of the day.

Drama

3 o'clock

Our class will be performing a play for the whole school next month. I am very excited. Today we start rehearsing. I play a queen, and my friend, Joanna plays a princess.

Going home time

Half-past 3
School is over now.
My Dad is already
waiting for me. He has
just been shopping!

Fun and games

4 o'clock
When we get back from school,
I play badminton in the garden
with my Dad.

What time do you finish school?

Time to go home

After an hour, Mum gets home from work. I tell her all about the bugs we found at school.

Dinner time

Half-past 5

I do my homework while Mum makes our dinner.

After dinner, we make plans for the **weekend**. I would like to go camping.

Time to get clean

6 o'clock

Before I go to bed,
I read a book.
Then I tidy my room
and have a bath.

Bedtime

Half-past 7

I had a great day
back at school.
Now I am very tired.

What time do you go to bed?

Time facts

We use clocks and watches to tell the time. Here are some other types of clocks that help us measure time.

Hourglass
The hourglass measures time with sand. The sand takes a certain amount of time to flow from one half of the hourglass to the other.

Sundial
The sundial has the same face as a clock. As the Sun moves across the sky, the shadow on the sundial moves too. The shadow points to the time.

Pocket watch

This watch got its name from its size. It is just small enough to fit into a pocket. The first pocket watch was made about 400 years ago.

Grandfather clock

This tall clock has a long **pendulum** that swings steadily.

What other types of clock have you seen?

Time to remember

Play this fun time game with a friend.

You need
A counter each and a dice.

How to play
The first person to throw a 6 starts. Take turns to throw the dice and move around the board. If you land on a star, follow the trail of stars up the board. If you land on a sad face, follow the arrow down the board. Try and tell the time on the clocks as you go along!

22

Start here

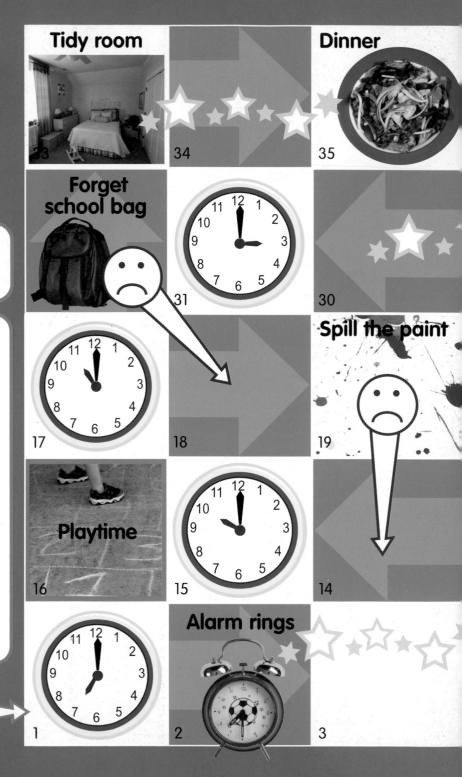

Tidy room — 33
34
Dinner — 35
Forget school bag — 31
30
17
18
Spill the paint — 19
Playtime — 16
15
14
1
Alarm rings — 2
3

Do homework

36

37

38 **Bath time**

Story time

39

40 **Go to sleep**

Help a friend

29

27

26

25

20

Lunchtime

21

22

23

24 **Work very hard**

Read book

PIRATES

13

12

11

Forgot homework

10

School starts

9

Eat breakfast

4

5

6

Catch the
7 **school bus**

8

Glossary

Do you remember what the times on these clocks are?

Afternoon Afternoon is the time between noon, or 12 o'clock, and dinner time.

Day A day is 24 hours. It starts and ends at midnight. It has a daytime and a night time. Daytime has four parts: morning, noon, afternoon and evening.

Half-past This is used when telling the time. It tells you that the big minute hand is pointing exactly at the six, and half of the hour has passed.

Hour An hour is 60 minutes. There are 24 hours in every day.

Minute A minute is 60 seconds. There are 60 minutes in an hour.

Morning Morning is the time between when you wake-up and noon.

O'Clock This is used when telling the time. It tells you that the big minute hand is pointing exactly at the 12 and the time is exactly the number the little hand is pointing at, such as 8 o'clock.

Pendulum A weight on a chain that some clocks use to help them show the correct time.

Week A week has seven days. They are Monday, Tuesday, Wednesday, Thursday, Friday, Saturday and Sunday.

Weekend The weekend is Saturday and Sunday.